The Distance Between Birds

poems by

Brooke McKinney

Finishing Line Press
Georgetown, Kentucky

The Distance Between Birds

Copyright © 2023 by Brooke McKinney
ISBN 979-8-88838-378-0 First Edition
All rights reserved under International and Pan-American Copyright Conventions. No part of this book may be reproduced in any manner whatsoever without written permission from the publisher, except in the case of brief quotations embodied in critical articles and reviews.

ACKNOWLEDGMENTS

Grateful acknowledgment is given to the following journals, where many of these poems and stories have appeared.

Montreal International Poetry Prize Anthology, "Half-Asleep in Daddy's War"
The Florida Review, "The Glass Jar Blues,"
Columbia Poetry Review, "The Tragedy of Light"
Salt Hill Journal, "Where We Live"
Potomac Review, "Boat Picture, You and Me"
Rhino Poetry, "Killing the Leaves"
Artemis, "The Distance Between Birds"
Kestrel, "Animal of Memory"
Poets.org, "Wild Misery"

Publisher: Leah Huete de Maines
Editor: Christen Kincaid
Cover Art: Alisha McKellar, AlishaMcKellar.com
Author Photo: Alisha McKellar
Cover Design: Jordan Roberts

Order online: www.finishinglinepress.com
also available on amazon.com

Author inquiries and mail orders:
Finishing Line Press
P. O. Box 1626
Georgetown, Kentucky 40324
U. S. A.

Table of Contents

The Tragedy of Light 1
Boat Picture, You and Me 2
Delphinium 3
This was a dream 4
Alzheimer's 5
What a Crow Said about War 6
Afterlife 7
Fledglings 8
A War that Keeps 9
The Glass Jar Blues 10
Some things only bloom after dark 11
Graveyard 12
Animal of Memory 13
Where We Live 14
Above us the birds sing 15
Killing the Leaves 17
The Hill 18
Starting Over 19
Half-Asleep in Daddy's War 20
The Distance Between Birds 22
Making a Bed from Memory 23
The Demolitionist 24

You're Still Not Immortal 25
Our Morning Game 26
Tangerine 27
Never Could Catch One 28
Familiar One 29
Love 30
Every Machine Breathes 31
Gardens of War 32
Longest Night of the Year, Family Court 33
Too Brief to Call it Home 34
 Heart Center, 7th Floor 35
Gardens 36
Wild Misery 37

*There are a thousand ways to kneel and kiss the ground;
there are a thousand ways to go home again.*
—Rumi

For Donald, Tommy, Jack and Jerry

The Tragedy of Light

I did not live long in sleep.

A dog's breath died around my ankles, the swallowing warmth staying there
    longer
than it should. The bedroom walls joined a kind of weakness, the way light
    survives
the riot of curtains, burrowing a wrinkle into my palm.

Isn't that how skin works?

The ashtray smells of old years and mistakes and the cracked fingers that held
    them.
If only I had one more cigarette, I could light it, saving it from tomorrow, then
the next. Mostly, I am useless. I tuck a leaf behind my ear, I point to birds in the
yard, I dig the earth for one worm, I trip over a rock that is you and say excuse
me for remembering.

But it's always the way light ruins me, landing on my skin like a boneless,
desperate bug. The way a day can bend itself into a perfect moon, erasing what
I know.

Boat Picture, You and Me

You're letting me drive the boat just this once. I'm steering.

You're holding a plastic cup of worms, a smile growing
beneath your sunglasses, a gold necklace dangling
from your neck—the one my mother gave you.

We were not sure of one another like stray dogs
who met in the alley—unwanted, not really interested.

I'm squinting my eyes, the sun pouring into them
like the idea of you being my father. I'd say it could have
been good by looking at this photo. The water waited for us
every fishing trip. Vietnam waited for you beneath that water,
shadows you meditated on for hours. A cigarette danced
between your lips, rolling from one corner to the other.

Love was something the world snatched from your hands
as if you were a child holding something you couldn't have.

War never ends, but I'm still confused why this photo
is the only time we ever loved one another. I'm okay
with that. I'm okay with this picture. I'm keeping it.

Delphinium

The florist asks, *what flowers would you like*
to wear in your hair for the wedding?

I think—*All of them!* But my head is not a garden
and cannot hold such beauty. Tulips will fall apart

before I can say, *I do.* Wedding means nothing
except it's something I must prepare for. *I want*

something blue, I say. Blue is a color I can rarely touch—
sky, ocean, feeling. *Delphinium,* she says, walking over

to a cooler, pulling a long stalk of blue bell-shaped blooms
from a bucket. The blooms are white at the stem, then bleed

into a soft blue. *Be careful,* she says, *they don't last long*
out of water. Like fish, I thought, which means they die.

They are beautiful, I want them in my hair, though she says
they might not live through a ceremony, my hair will be their grave.

On the way home, I hold them in my lap, they wilt. I revive them
in a cup of water in the kitchen windowsill. I expect them to die

by morning. I look up delphinium to search for its meaning.
It symbolizes an "open heart" but if ingested, toxic to humans.

A year later, still no wedding. The delphinium is alive, blooming
downward into eternity. It's a sad thing, but it's not dead.

I call the florist and say, *you were wrong, one year later*
and they're still here, but I'm not sure I can say the same about love.

This was a dream

I held the dandelion to my lips
and with my lungs gave it a kind of death,

in which its head scattered into pieces,
seeds flying through the wind, but in the end,

it all came back together on the earth
again, into its refuge. I repeated the death,

over and over, until I understood this sad story.

Alzheimer's

His eyes bounce
all ways in his head
like he doesn't know
he's inside himself—

*Can't escape what you are
even if you've lost it.*

He builds secrets,
talking his fingers
into doing something.

If one muscle hears him,
he can go back fixing cars,
go back to holding the woman
he loved, the woman that dies
each morning he wakes up.

What he can't forget
is closest to him, the war
and its evening sun stroking

the tops of canopies,
only a sliver of light breaking
through the leaves,
landing
on his face.

What a Crow Said about War

The crow is a bird of years,
time hidden in each lost feather

tucked into the wind.
Perched on the headstone

above your name, black wings cover
the soft edges of a fresh grave.

The crow builds a path
through the sky, returning to the same

places—fences, white lines
of highways, low branches

of trees, hanging on the edge
of tragedy. I know of at least one

crow that witnessed an entire war,
watching from above and below.

Killing is the same no matter
from what direction you look.

Afterlife

The leaves rustle and I toss
your name like a blossom

into the afterlife of rain. It echoes
the way the lost call of a hawk travels

a perching silence of trees.

I recall you like a mother
lion or desperate wind, nervous love

hanging on the back of the neck.
I named a leaf after you the day

you died. Within hours
it shriveled, broke into a brittle

song of jagged yellow and red.
I placed it in my palm thinking

if I held it, there'd be no flying away.

Fledglings

On cold days, robins leave behind
their dead as winter builds its hive
of survival. I think of my father
who never held me in the warmth
of his palm.

Arranging the mornings
are difficult—I reach for the window,
press my ear to the screen, where I hear
robins talking in and out of the branches.

How do they live a life full of need,
not having to map a home from nest to sky,
not knowing the fathers who left them
in corners of trees.

A War that Keeps

I hope that when you died you didn't
go back to Vietnam like your brother,
how he stumbled with a body of bones
to the front yard the night he died, falling
to his knees, crawling into a family of boxwoods.

He squirmed in the muddy heart of his mother's
garden, a cigarette hung, half-lit, wet from a sprinkler
slapping him in the face. When you reached
for his wilted human shell, he cried, refusing
to move, afraid of the jungle growing around him.

He yelled, *Ceasefire!* You fell with him,
but this time, it wasn't the cancer, it was what
the war kept inside him, kept rocking him
around his body, his body gone
with a memory he'd never catch up with.

The Glass Jar Blues

I keep an animal in a glass jar. You can see
it rocking around, searching for air or one small wind.

I have poked holes in the top, so it can breathe
or just rise to the idea of breathing. I put leaves

in the jar to make love exist and a stick so that it has hope
to climb out of its infinite pain. There's enough water

to crown the bottom of the jar so it may wet its feet
and there's a rock so it can sit and think—anything trapped

needs a place to think. I watch it struggle every day, trying
to escape. I walk over to comfort it, tapping my finger

on the glass, saying things—*it's going to be fine, I know
you are not happy, but you are safe.*

Some things only bloom after dark

Like the heart dividing,
breaking in half, beating in unison—
anything not born yet is already
with the birds shackled to a hollow sky.

Tell me, will you ever be in love?

I'm afraid your body will never move
again. It looks like an empty doll
spread over the white sheets, the hospital
bed tilted for your lungs to breathe.

For a second, I see myself running around
the sterile room, planting ceramic pots
full of moonflowers, to show you hope comes
from other things besides prayer and luck,
that darkness, too, can wake the sleeping.

Your heart monitor keeps me awake,
I'm making note each beep and ding
but for each sliver of silence, I pause,
wide-eyed I jump and wake you—
*Look, look at the moon, it's shining
and full and bright like a flower.*

Graveyard

These tulip bodies
will never fall to the earth—
Death has no garden

Animal of Memory

If only I had the child's brain, full to the skull of those blessed enzymes, allowing the animal to forget.

I want to forget the way morning rolls over on its back and night is gone.

I could nest in the eyes of an old woman, hollow in the habits of her rocking chair or in the photograph of the man she says went to war in a moaning wind and how she never checked the weather after that. She never saw that wind again. Her heart is mostly bone now, buried in a back room between her breasts, dangling for something to bite it, but nothing comes around hungry anymore.

I want to forget the way dandelions do when their heads are blown off by the storm of a human breath.

I want to forget the man whose hair I never got to see turn gray. The man who is a father. The man who is a father who just showed up after I lost the child's power to forget.

Where We Live

The snow left and I wanted to tell you
how delicate it was. How a little drop

of blood can ruin a yard covered in white.
The night swallowed and hummed

its way into a back room of old stars,
their soft bodies wilt into white smoke.

I think it is something more secret than us,
becoming one brief hour after another.

Bodies want to know other bodies, sleeping
in the grass beneath irises. They want to be

in conversation with something smaller
than themselves. Perhaps the cardinal empty of life

will know the sky is no home at all.
Maybe you still live in Long Bình.

Maybe that is your sky now, your home
a winter inside you, releasing its jaws.

Above us the birds sing

The gift of having you
one more day is a reminder
that one day I will not.

We sit in the garden, morning
sun gives your body a sure sign
of life. Your eyes are closed, I watch

shadows of birds fly through
your white fur, the black dot
on your head is a souvenir of how

we met thirteen years ago.
I hear church bells in the distance,
they add some kind of charm

to our routine—wake up, breathe,
enjoy whatever time is left, breathe
again, sleep, please breathe, again.
I want to reach down, touch you,
hold your paw, trace the black dot
over and over as if to erase it,
bring it back, erase it, but I don't.

Even a dog knows what is lost
Even a dog knows bird song
Even a dog knows war is hell

I want to readjust your back legs
since a disease has hindered you to do it
yourself or maybe I'll pop another pill
down your throat to ensure
the tumor is not bleeding.

Oh, my sweet boy, my sweet boy,
how beautiful the world is around us
for such ugly things to be inside you,

taking you further and further away
from me. Come back to me and the birds
and the sun and the worm that curves
so softly into itself, into the dirt,
just below where you lie.

Killing the Leaves

I don't guess I'll ever get over that child saving me from becoming a pile of meat and blood. The streets covered in urine and blood, anyway.

You'd think these roads were nothing but remains of humans once in love. I wrote notes on the back of cigarettes and coined a new term for help—please.

The trees were dying quicker than we were, spraying for mosquitoes, killing the leaves becoming lungs becoming leaves becoming stiff.

Now that I'm back home, I want to shoot my daddy, though his name isn't Charlie. I thank mama for having a stroke—saving me from the filth of the frontline.

Driving home sometimes, the sunset stands down behind the trees, bursting into a thousand fires between those veins of branches, killing the leaves in the rear-view mirror…

I hit the brakes. I yell, Ceasefire! Goddamn that sticker—*Objects in the mirror are closer than they appear.*

The Hill

Broken, clay pots relax side by side,
a fake iris sleeps, dreaming
the memories of what's dead.

One day the world will be this—
a bed of soldiers, struggling to keep
their names above dirt.

Starting Over

So much of our lives are starting
over. Waking in the mornings, the same
sun pouring through the curtains, the same
shoes and car and road taking us
to the job that chews away our hours.
The meals we prepare, yards we mow, the same
tulips that bloom and then go to die.
But tonight, we walk up Woods Bridge,
crossing the Beaufort River, the crescent moon
shaped like our tired eyes. The black water
crashes beneath us as we sneak
up on the egrets. They feel us, taking flight
from the orange glow of the bridge, disappearing
into the dark marsh, only moonlight shining
off their feathered backs.

Across the bridge and back, starting
over, starting over.

We walk beneath the oaks, Spanish moss
hanging like ghosts, reaching down to touch
the living. I do not mind it. I do not
mind this path. We must learn to see everything
as new, inviting us to know it. We must look
at the faces of our loved ones everyday
as if it were the first time.

Half-Asleep in Daddy's War

And all our dreams will roll toward the hunt,
some half-asleep dogs mingling behind doors.
My family swallows a habit of barbiturates—
the old spores of war, last years of crumbling
leaves. The wind comes back for us. It stalks.
Whose lungs cracked open in a dream wheezing?

What kind of wind goes off wheezing?
Half-asleep dogs come out of doors to hunt
Our dream comes back for us. It stalks.
My family keeps a habit of closing doors,
memories of Vietnam come back crumbling
and years have a way of keeping us on barbiturates.

This dream is a body full of barbiturates.
How do sleeping dogs die without wheezing?
We bring back to the dark a habit of crumbling
lungs half-asleep after returning from the hunt.
To believe this family can still walk through doors,
smelling the odor of war, it's moldy body. It stalks.

And all of memory will follow us dead. It stalks.
We can't help but beg for our barbiturates
and now the family must lock all their doors
or else nothing is free from the wheezing.
The wind finds a way to carry us back to hunt
as dogs go off again into a dream that's crumbling.

We can't keep us here in a body still crumbling.
There's a love that war stole and it's here. It stalks.
The same way the dogs dig up bones from the hunt
and, no, we can't stop our family tradition of barbiturates.
But don't we lie down sometimes to feel the wheezing?
Sometimes we rise again and open a few doors.

The wind has brought something to our doors—
A memory stacked memory, and oh, its crumbling.

Will silence come and take away this wheezing?
The family thinks the war is gone. It's back. It stalks.
We think we are safe because we are fed by barbiturates
so let's go now into the mind and bring back the hunt.

Wheezing, it sounds like the opening of doors
and we forget the crumbling that wakes us to hunt
We hold on to our barbiturates—afraid of what stalks.

The Distance Between Birds

You've thought about the oak
outliving the war and how you won't.

How your mother cracked an egg
over a bowl, yellow spilling over
her as another dying day.

Like the six-day-old pear
on the counter, you ripen
and rot at the same time.

You've thought about the distance
between birds. How they know
when to settle the fracture.

Souvenirs from Vietnam were kept
in your lungs and head, sometimes you

still confuse a stranger for a stranger.
The want to erase each one
tunneled inside skin and mind.

You've thought about the oak
outliving you and how *this* war won't.

Making a Bed from Memory

On grandmother's ninetieth birthday
we could only fit so many candles on the cake—
Age will set you on fire if you're not careful.

She looked like a mama wolf, her hair
a wind-curled fur streaked black and white.
Her eyes fed us a kind of wisdom
we knew not to use before the night
was over. We'd have none left by morning
anyway, she told us. Now, when I see

her she's so blind, making her bed is all
she can do in one day. She knows
where the corners fall, where fingers bend,
where touch has been over and over again.

The Demolitionist

You run toward the sun
wanting to be taken down with it.

The air tastes like blood
if you can believe such a thing.

The mud becomes bodies becomes
a decaying becomes a new earth.

The tangerine trees burst and die, fall
like confetti, but this isn't

a celebration unless death is

You're Still Not Immortal

Listen now

to the clock, little

hands moving time

around in a circle,

measuring your life

on a kitchen wall.

Our Morning Game

The robins come again. I toss them
what's left of my *brain
food*—nuts, seeds.

They are not hungry, they want
to play. I chase them
from the porch, trying to guess
where they will land.

A robin does not fly far
from the ground and I wonder
if it knows the significance of wings,

if it knows how far it can go. I run
after them again as they glide a little
over the earth, landing only steps

in front of me. I do this again,
again until I push them back
into the trees where they perch

on the lowest branch.
A hawk passes by and warns
the world—its wings more broken-in

than a robin's. I watch
as the robins go lower, lower
to earth as if burying themselves

into a life without feathers. I stand
alone in one place. I watch the hawk
circle the path its body has been

through over and over in the sky.
I step back, I step back,
I step back, realizing I am
not a bird in this game.

Tangerine

You run toward the sun
wanting to be taken down with it.

The air tastes like blood
if you can believe such a thing.

The mud becomes bodies becomes
a decaying becomes a new earth.

The tangerine trees burst and die, fall
like confetti, but this isn't

a celebration unless death is.

Never Could Catch One

There stood a girl with clothes
too small, yellow skirt is all.

I can remember her digging up
a mountain of junk for something to eat.

One pill a day, kept malaria out
of my blood, enough for Agent Orange

to creep in. Four or five months later
you didn't care if you died or not.

They told me—*Do like the others do. Pray
a little bit.* I did, the night before

I piled bodies on top of bodies you
could only see the pile as one body. I watched

women drop bombs from their bras,
watched lonely men die.

In Vietnam, they had lizards the size
of alligators in Georgia. *I never could catch one.*

Familiar One

The wind brings a hundred robins—

They put their red breasted bodies
against other bodies. One leans into a bush,
one settles by the tire of a parked Jeep.

One gives its feathers away to another bird.

Robins are not listening for worms
when they cock their heads to one side,

they are searching for a window, a reflection
to plant their eyes inside. And once they see themselves,
they can be heard singing all day long.

Love

A cardinal flies
by, followed by another—
Love will not save me.

Every Machine Breathes

Lungs shrivel, bend into half-moons,
burrowing between your breasts
as cancer naps in cocoons—
little souvenirs of war. Each breath is
a bullet in the wind, memories of a mother

Caution is the art of cracking an egg
she said, watching yellow spill
over her tired fingers into a bowl,

reminding you of the jungle's evening sun
sinking into a horizon of young men,
photographs of lovers tucked in helmets.

Mud spreads itself like a home
of doves mapping a path to the sky.
Love is the art of surviving a war
she said, a soldier's dance fades
beneath a dusk so soft it can't be seen.

Gardens of War

I.
A poppy grows up
unearthed inside a worm's thought—
red as any heart

        II.
        The dirt frees crimson
        buds lining fields of crosses—
        a lost soldier's love

III.
Mud stirs beneath them,
growing near home, forgotten
poppies breed again

        IV.
        A wooden cross speaks
        as dirt delivers stories
        no flower can tell

Longest Night of the Year, Family Court

The violin's melancholic cry is coming
from the back room, the cat is curling
into himself like the ouroboros,
a thousand-year-old soul made of grey
fur, soft from the years and years of hands
that have loved him. It is cold tonight,
the rain is cold tonight, and so,
he sleeps in a chair, comforted
by the warmth of December dreams.
Tonight, we live farthest from the sun,
light scattering, tucking itself away
into all corners of the Earth, darkness falling
here where folders stack like wood,
folders full of children we will never know.
It is the longest night of the year,
these children will dream of snow,
dream of Christmas because they are still
young and fit for imagination, they will dream
of things we will never know. They will dream
on into this night, long and absent of light,
the cat will dream what cats dream of
and the violin, oh the violin, it will not sleep tonight.

Too Brief to Call it Home

A low wind came, plucking heads
off tulips that just opened yesterday

and I believe it's something happening
in all corners of the world—beauty

shattered by beauty. It is not weather
that moves me toward shelter, not the rain,

or even the darkness, but a small light
of choice that hangs on the tail of memory

and I'm afraid I'm not animal enough
to shake it off. I am lonely for nothing.

Death is petal by petal for a tulip, as soon
as it invites one sigh. I touch it,

its softness the most finite thing—
ash that can't be put back together.

Heart center, 7th Floor

You asked for morphine—*I want
to forget as much as this as I can.*

The foothills of Georgia mountains
surrounded you. The heart tower peaked,
a window gave you rain clouds, bolts
of lightening and a hawk, you watched
soar in and out of the glass frame,

keeping your eye on it until the morphine
put you back to sleep.

A bag of your things sat next to me
on the stiff couch. It smelled like cigarettes.
All the things they stripped off you
when you arrived—plaid snap button shirt,
Levi's, nasal spray, baseball cap,
a canned ginger ale, Winstons, a lighter,
a few dimes and pennies, your teeth.

You popped back up, surprised again
where you were. *Where did my hawk go?*

You said it was there to protect you, to bring you
wisdom, you went back to sleep for a minute or two.

Woke again—*You know this aneurysm on my heart
could blow any second?* Your eyes moved back
to the window, rain coming down hard. For a minute,
you thought we were so high we were above the birds,
but then that hawk passed
over just above us on the seventh floor.
No, you said. *That's good. Looks like we're still below the birds.*

Gardens

Birds fly, anxious, by
the immortal irises
resting beneath them

Wild Misery

"Is there no way out of the mind?"
—Sylvia Plath

Driving by the cemetery I see
a detour sign by the front gate as if

there is an alternative so I park
by the gate, shut my eyes and I can feel

flooding in the earth's throat, swallowing the
long way home. I'm feeding my head. I am

putting the birds up to sleep, pretending
I've never seen a mannequin, a door,

a building, I desire horizontal
things in the distance—my bones

sinking, side to side like air, a faded
map or some heavy confetti for the

animals to consider. *I am so anticlimactic compared
to birds,* the juxtaposition of heart

and dirt, lying down feels good, being flat
and all that… then I take up rocks, tulips,

and old stories, toss them, assemble them
like stars, all sad and sharp as if I just

took all the frontal lobotomies in
the world and put back together one hell

of a human, but hell is finding out
you are a wild misery. It must be

difficult for a god to raise a hand
and say—*I didn't do it. I didn't*

create a detour for you. So where did
I think I was going today? To talk

with some natural stranger hidden
beneath all the mud, stone, and story? But

I have decided what to do. I will
invite winter to live inside me, my

mother, a tree dying to become anything
but a pile of branches even if there is

no internal evidence of the monotonous
hum coming from outside. The birds are up.

I think that is enough.

Brooke McKinney is a poet and writer from South Georgia. She earned her Bachelor of Arts in English from Valdosta State University and holds an MFA in Creative Writing from Hollins University. Her work has received scholarships to the Sewanee Writers' Conference, Looking Glass Rock Writers' Conference, and Writers in Paradise. She is also the recipient of two Academy of American Poets Awards. Her work has appeared or is forthcoming in *The Florida Review, New South, Salt Hill Journal, Potomac Review, The Southeast Review, Columbia Poetry Review, RHINO Poetry,* and *the Montreal International Poetry Prize Anthology.* She lives with two dogs, Jane and Arlo.

www.ingramcontent.com/pod-product-compliance
Lightning Source LLC
Chambersburg PA
CBHW020343170426
43200CB00006B/491